PHOTOSHOP
FOR
BEGINNERS
(BOOK 2)

An extensive guide to learning the basics of Photoshop

Brian Indigo

Table of Content

Introduction

The topic of learning fundamental background methods is finished in the second book of "Photoshop for Beginners." By providing aspiring photographers with the tools and knowledge they need to enhance their Photoshop skills, this portion builds on the foundation laid in Book One.

This chapter of the book will take you on a transformative journey through the subtleties of a professional-caliber comprehension of the fundamentals of Photoshop. You may learn the fundamentals of Photoshop in this section and unleash your creativity. You can achieve this by getting a better understanding of documents, Photoshop's tools and functions, and potential user modifications.

We go fully into the area of documents, the capabilities, and features of Photoshop, personalization, keyboard shortcuts, and many other topics.

By the end of Book Two, you will possess a broad variety of abilities in the fundamentals of Photoshop.

Chapter 1

Photoshop Document Creation and Opening

The method for generating new documents and opening old ones in Photoshop is simple. Here are how to create and open documents in Photoshop, whether you're beginning a new project or editing one that already exists:

A New Document to Be Created:

- ❖ Open Photoshop on your PC to start the program. It is often located in your Start menu (Windows) or Applications folder (Mac).

- ❖ Go to File > New by clicking on "File" in the top menu bar and choosing "New."

As an alternative, you may use Ctrl+N on a Windows or Mac computer.

A document's properties are set:

❖ The properties of your new document may be specified using the dialog box that will display. You may choose the document's resolution, color mode, width, height, and background information here. According to the needs of your project, adjust these values.

❖ After configuring the document's settings, click the "Create" button. The options you choose will be used by Photoshop to generate a new document. Your brand-new document will be represented by a brand-new tab in the workspace.

Opening a Current Document:

❖ Click File > Open: To open a previously saved document, click File in the menu bar and then choose "Open." As an alternative, you may use Ctrl+O on a Windows or Mac computer.

Search for the File:

❖ The file you wish to open may be found by browsing the folders on your computer using the dialog box that will display. Click the "Open" button after navigating to the folder containing the file and selecting it.

❖ Document Opens in Photoshop: After you've chosen the file, Photoshop will open it in a brand-new tab in your workspace. The document's contents are now available for viewing and editing.

❖ It's crucial to remember that Photoshop is compatible with a wide variety of file types, including PSD (the native format of Photoshop), JPEG, PNG, TIFF, and many more. Make that a file can be opened in Photoshop by checking its compatibility or, if necessary, converting it to a recognized format.

Photoshop: Making a New Document with Specific Dimensions and Settings

The instructions below will show you how to create a new document in Photoshop with the size and settings your project demands:

❖ Open Photoshop on your PC to start the program. It may be found on your Mac in the Applications folder or on Windows in the Start menu.

❖ Go to File > New
by clicking on "File" in the top menu bar and choosing "New." As an alternative, you may use *Ctrl+N* on a Windows or Mac computer.

Property settings are made for a document:

The properties of your new document may be specified using the dialog box that will display. Here is how to set up the settings:

❖ Name your document by entering a name. You may subsequently recognize it thanks to this.

❖ **Preset:** Select a preset from the drop-down menu, to begin with predetermined parameters. Alternatively, choose "Custom" to establish your own preferences.

❖ **Width and Height:** Indicate your document's measurements in pixels, inches, centimeters, millimeters, points, or picas. A measuring unit may be chosen from a drop-down menu or you can input numbers for width and height separately.

❖ **Resolution:** Decide how high or low your document should be. 72 pixels per inch (PPI) is the industry standard for online or screen-based designs, whereas 300 PPI is often utilized for print projects.

- ❖ **Color Mode:** Determine the best color mode for your project based on its specifications. While CMYK is preferable for print, RGB is often utilized for digital designs.

- ❖ **Backdrop Contents:** Pick the initial backdrop for your documents, such as a translucent background, a white background, or any other background color you want.

- ❖ If necessary, you may access other parameters like color profile, bit depth, and pixel aspect ratio by clicking the "Advanced" button. Adapt these variables to the needs of your particular project.

After making all the necessary configurations, choose "Create" by clicking the button. Based on the chosen parameters and dimensions, Photoshop will create a new document. The workspace will now have a brand-new tab for your freshly generated document.

Opening Current Documents and Images in Photoshop

To modify or make further changes to existing photos or documents in Photoshop, just follow these easy steps:

❖ Open Photoshop on your PC to start the program. It may be found on your Mac in the Applications folder or on Windows in the Start menu.

- ❖ **Go to File > Open**

  by clicking on "File" in the top menu bar and choosing "Open." Alternatively, you may use Ctrl+O on a Windows or Mac computer.

- ❖ **Find the Image or Document:** A dialog box enabling you to search through the folders on your computer and find the image or document you wish to open will appear. The file's location may be found by visiting the directory.

- ❖ **Pick the file:**
- ❖ When you've found the file, click it to choose it.
- ❖ **Click "Open" to begin:** After choosing the file, click "Open." Now, Photoshop will load the picture or file into its workspace.

❖ **Document Opens in Photoshop:** The document or picture you choose will appear in a new tab inside the Photoshop workspace. Its contents may now be viewed and modified as needed.

❖ Photoshop supports a wide range of file types, including JPEG, PNG, TIFF, PSD (the original Photoshop format), and many more. Make that a file can be opened in Photoshop by checking its compatibility or, if necessary, converting it to a recognized format.

By following these instructions, you may open existing photos or documents in Photoshop with ease, giving you the ability to edit, improve, or modify your files as needed utilizing the software's extensive set of tools and functions.

Understanding Resolution and Color Modes' Importance in Photoshop

The two most important components of dealing with photos in Photoshop are resolution and color modes. They have a big impact on how good, clear, and accurate your designs' colors are. Let's go further into their significance:

- ❖ The resolution of a picture, measured in pixels per inch (PPI), directly affects its degree of sharpness and detail. When producing or altering photographs in Photoshop for print or digital usage, the resolution is essential.

- ❖ **Print Projects:** A greater resolution is often needed when creating designs for printed products like brochures, flyers, or posters. A print resolution of 300 PPI (pixels per inch) is considered typical. When printing the design, sharp details and seamless transitions are ensured by higher resolution.

❖ **Digital Projects:** A lower resolution of 72 PPI is often utilized for online graphics or screen-based designs. This resolution offers the best clarity and file size for online viewing since digital screens have lower pixel densities than print.

P.S. To prevent pixelation or quality loss when resizing or printing your photographs, it's crucial to establish the right resolution from the start.

❖ **Color modes:** These settings define how colors are displayed and represented in a picture. There are many color modes that

Photoshop provides, each useful for a particular task:

Note: Digital projects and web-based designs generally employ the RGB (Red, Green, Blue) color mode. By blending various red, green, and blue light intensities, RGB generates colors. It provides a wide variety of vivid colors that are appropriate for displays and digital media.

Note: The color mode used for print projects is CMYK (Cyan, Magenta, Yellow, Black). By blending different intensities of cyan, magenta, yellow, and black inks, it simulates color. In order to accommodate for the color restrictions of the printing process, CMYK offers the correct color representation for printing.

❖ **Grayscale:** The grayscale mode completely removes the color information from a picture and instead represents it using various degrees of gray. For black-and-white images or to achieve a particular aesthetic impression, it is often utilized.

NOTE:

❖ It is essential to choose the proper color mode in order to guarantee color accuracy and consistency across various media. It's crucial to choose the correct color mode from the outset since switching a picture between color modes might cause color shifts or information loss.

❖ You can make sure that your photographs are of the greatest quality and appropriate for their intended purpose, whether it's for print or digital media, by knowing the significance of resolution and color settings in Photoshop. The overall visual impact and professionalism of your designs are influenced by the resolution and color mode options that you choose.

Chapter 2

Basic Photoshop Tools and Features

You may edit and modify your photographs using Photoshop's extensive set of tools and features with both accuracy and originality. The following are some crucial devices and operations you should get acquainted with:

Choice Instruments:

- ❖ **Marquee Tools:** You may choose to use the rectangular, elliptical, or single-row/column marquee tools.
- ❖ **Lasso Tools:** Allows for freehand or edge-based selections.
- ❖ **Magic Wand Tool:** Using the Magic Wand tool, you may quickly choose pixels with related hues or tones.

- ❖ **Quick Selection Tool:** With the help of the Quick Selection Tool, related regions are automatically selected.

Tools for correction and retouching

- ❖ **Clone Stamp Tool:** Useful for deleting undesired items, it copies pixels from one region and applies them to another.
- ❖ **Healing Brush Tool:** Utilizing the surrounding pixels, the healing brush tool smoothes out flaws.
- ❖ **Spot Healing Brush Tool:** Easily gets rid of blemishes or other minor flaws.
- ❖ **material-Aware Fill:** Automatically inserts material into pre-selected regions depending on the pixels around it.

Tool for painting with a brush:

- ❖ **Brush Tool:** You may paint or draw using various brush defaults and settings with the brush tool.

❖ **The Eraser Tool:** removes pixels and enables targeted erasure or modification.

❖ **Gradient Tool:** Produces seamless color gradients.

❖ **Paint Bucket Tool:** Fills a chosen area with a solid color or pattern using the paint bucket tool.

Tools for transformation:

❖ **Move Tool:** Repositions and moves the layers or items you want.

❖ **Crop Tool:** Image size or aspect ratios may be changed with the crop tool.

❖ **Transform Tool:** You may scale, rotate, skew, or deform items with the transform tool.

Tools for Using Layers and Masks:

❖ **Layer Panel:** Controls layer visibility and blending modes using the layer panel.

- ❖ **Layer Mask:** Selected areas of a layer may be selectively hidden or shown.
- ❖ **Adjustment Layers:** Use adjustment layers to make non-destructive changes to pictures' color, brightness, and other aspects.

Tools for text and typography:

- ❖ **Type Tool:** Add and modify text in your compositions with the type tool.
- ❖ **Character and Paragraph Panel:** Customize text properties including font, size, alignment, and spacing using the character and paragraph panels.

Effects and Filters:

- ❖ **Filter Gallery:** Apply many artistic and creative effects to your photographs with the filter gallery.

- ❖ **Blur, Sharpen, and Smudge:** Use the tools to enhance or soften certain areas: blur, sharpen, and smudge.
- ❖ **Layer Styles:** Drop shadows, gradients, bevels, and other effects may be added to layers using layer styles.

These are only a handful of the crucial features and tools offered by Photoshop. You'll find even more tools and approaches that may help you get the outcomes you want as you investigate and practice. To make your photographs come to life, don't be afraid to try new things, make use of Photoshop's powerful toolkit, and let your imagination run wild.

Mastering ChatGPT's Keyboard Shortcuts for Effective Workflow

In Photoshop, keyboard shortcuts are quite helpful since they speed up your workflow, save you time, and increase productivity. You should become proficient in the following keyboard shortcuts in order to operate in Photoshop more quickly:

Choice and Navigation:

- ❖ **V:** To make manipulating objects simple, use the Move Tool.
- ❖ **Ctrl or Cmd + D:** Deselect any currently selected item using Ctrl or Cmd + D.
- ❖ **Ctrl/Cmd + Z:** Reverse your most recent action.
- ❖ **Spacebar:** Temporarily turn on the Hand Tool for picture navigation.

- ❖ **Ctrl or Cmd plus "+/-":** To zoom in or out of your picture, use Ctrl or Cmd plus "+/-".

Tools and Purposes:

- ❖ **B:** To paint or retouch, turn on the Brush Tool.
- ❖ **E:** Choose the Eraser Tool to eliminate pixels or make fine modifications.
- ❖ **J:** To remove flaws or blemishes, use the Healing Brush Tool.
- ❖ **M:** Select items by using the Marquee Tool.
- ❖ **T:** Use the Text Tool to enter and modify text.

Adjusting and Layering:

- ❖ **Ctrl/Cmd + J:** Duplicate the layer you've chosen with Ctrl/Cmd + J.
- ❖ **Ctrl or Cmd + G:** To group selected layers into a folder, use Ctrl or Cmd + G.

- ❖ **Ctrl/Cmd + T:** To scale, rotate, or distort layers, use the keyboard shortcut Ctrl/Cmd + T.
- ❖ **Ctrl or Cmd + U:** Open the Hue or Saturation adjustment panel using the keys Ctrl or Cmd + U.
- ❖ **Ctrl or Cmd + L:** Open the Levels adjustment panel by pressing Ctrl or Cmd + L.

Miscellaneous:

- ❖ **Ctrl or Cmd + S:** To save your work, use Ctrl or Cmd + S.
- ❖ **Ctrl/Cmd + Shift + N:** New layer creation using Ctrl/Cmd + Shift + N.
- ❖ **Ctrl/Cmd + Alt + Z:** Press the keys Ctrl/Cmd + Alt + Z to repeatedly go back in the history panel.
- ❖ **Ctrl/Cmd + Shift + S:** Save your work in a new file format by using the keys Ctrl/Cmd + Shift + S.

❖ **Ctrl/Cmd + Alt + Shift + E:** Merge all visible layers into a new layer by pressing Ctrl/Cmd + Alt + Shift + E.

Chapter 3

Photoshop Preferences Customization

Changing Photoshop's options enables you to adapt the program to your own requirements and preferences. The following areas if preferred may be modified;

Generally Speaking:

- ❖ **Interface Color:** Choose between a deeper color scheme or the usual light gray for the interface.
- ❖ **Cursor options:** Change the cursor's size, shape, and other characteristics.
- ❖ **shortcuts on the keyboard:** Create new keyboard shortcuts or modify existing ones for different tasks.

❖ **File management:** Configure the auto-recovery, file compatibility, and file-saving parameters.

Preferences for tools:

❖ Individual tools, such as the Brush Tool, Crop Tool, or Healing Brush Tool, may have their behavior and look altered.

❖ A tool's parameters may be changed, including the brush size, opacity, blending modes, and more.

Preferences for Performance:

❖ Adapt memory allocation and cache settings to your computer's specs to improve performance.

❖ To maximize the performance of the graphics processing unit, alter the GPU settings.

❖ To balance speed and file size, enable or deactivate features like History States and Cache Levels.

Preferences for Interfaces

❖ Panels, menus, and toolbars may all be customized in terms of design and placement.

❖ Establish preferences for workspace organization, screen modes, and other interface-related options.

❖ Change the way certain components, including text size, icon size, or thumbnail quality, look.

Preferences for Units & Rulers:

❖ Give the rulers, type, and other items' units of measurement.

❖ Set the new documents' default resolution.

❖ Configure the grid and guidelines for exact alignment and layout.

P.S: In Photoshop, pick "Preferences" from the "Edit" menu (Windows) or "Photoshop" menu (Mac) to access and modify preferences. From there, you may explore the many preference categories and change things to suit your tastes.

Adapting Photoshop's Settings to Your Needs

Utilizing Photoshop's flexibility to be customized to fit your own tastes and workflow is one of its many benefits. The following are some crucial places where you may adjust settings to meet your needs:

Space Organization:

❖ Drag and drop panels and toolbars into the desired positions to arrange them in a way that best suits your working style. Related panels may be grouped together, collapsed or expanded, and docked in various locations.

❖ When you have your panels and toolbars in the proper order, save the customized workspace configuration. Workspaces may then be loaded. Afterward, you may move between several stored workspaces based on the project or job you're working on.

Keyboard shortcuts:

❖ Access the Keyboard Shortcuts box to alter or create keyboard shortcuts for a variety of tasks and tools. To expedite your process, provide shortcuts to commonly used functions.

❖ Shortcut settings may be exported and imported onto other computers if you transfer computers or want to share your personalized shortcuts with others.

Preferences:

❖ **General Preferences:** Tailor the color of the interface, the way the cursor behaves, and the file management choices to your tastes.

❖ **Tools Preferences:** Tailor each tool's parameters to your preferences for more effective editing by changing things like brush size, opacity, and blending modes.

❖ **Performance Preferences:** Depending on the capabilities of your machine, allocate RAM, modify cache settings, and use GPU acceleration to maximize performance.

❖ **Interface Preferences:** Create an interface that works best for you by modifying the design and organization of panels, menus, and toolbars.

Presets:

❖ **Brush Presets:** Create and store personalized brush presets with precise parameters for size, hardness, and opacity to have easy access to your preferred brushes.

❖ **Layer, Styles, and Effects:** The effects and styles of layers To ensure consistency between projects, save and reuse layer styles like gradients or drop shadows.

❖ **Custom Shapes:** Create and store your own unique shapes for simple usage in various applications.

Changing Preferences for File Handling, Performance, and Interface

To improve speed, personalize the interface, and control file management in Photoshop, you have the freedom to change a variety of parameters. Here are some significant preferences you may change:

Favorite Performances:

❖ **Memory Usage:** Increase Photoshop's memory allocation to improve performance. Depending on the RAM your machine has available, adjust the "Let Photoshop Use" slider.

❖ **Graphics Processor Settings:** Configuring the graphics processor Make use of the graphics processing unit (GPU) capability of your computer to accelerate rendering and display chores.

If your computer can handle it, turn on GPU acceleration.

- ❖ **History & Cache:** To limit how many actions you may undo, choose the amount of History States. For better zooming and brush strokes, balance performance and file size by adjusting the cache levels.

Preferences In terms of interfaces

- ❖ **Appearance:** Make the Photoshop interface's color scheme your own. Choose a bright, medium, or dark UI to fit your visual tastes.
- ❖ **Panels:** Group, dock, and arrange panels to set up your workplace in a way that best matches your workflow. You may customize panel configurations, collapse or extend panels, and save them as workplaces for easy access.

- ❖ **Font Size:** Change the font size to make the user interface text easier to read and more pleasant to use.

- ❖ **Display Modes:** Set the preferred screen mode, such as Standard Screen Mode, Full Screen Mode with Menu Bar, or Full-Screen Mode, for working with and opening documents.

Preferences for file handling:

- ❖ **File Saving Options:** Customize how Photoshop stores files using the file-saving options. Depending on your demands, choose the file formats, compatibility choices, and compression levels.

- ❖ **File Auto Recovery:** Enable file auto-recovery to automatically save your work at regular intervals and lessen the chance of data loss in the event of a breakdown or power outage.

P.S: Select "Preferences" from the "Edit" menu on Windows or the "Photoshop" menu on a Mac to access these settings. Visit the appropriate areas, such as Performance, Interface, and File Handling, to make the necessary modifications.

Custom Workspaces and Keyboard Shortcuts Configuration

To streamline your work and increase productivity in Photoshop, you may set up unique keyboard shortcuts and design unique workspaces. How to accomplish it is as follows:

Conclusion

"Photoshop for Beginners" (Book 2) Will Help You Take Your Photoshop Skills to New Heights.

Thank you for finishing Book 2 of "Photoshop for Beginners"! You have developed a whole new level of Photoshop proficiency, and you are now armed with sophisticated methods and information that will make you stand out in the field of digital art.

With every new chapter, you have become more self-assured and adept in using Photoshop's robust tools, enabling you to express your creative vision with accuracy and grace. You now possess the skills necessary to produce captivating and motivating images.

You will be proud of how far you have come as you think back on your time with Photoshop for Beginners (book 2). You have embraced the power of Photoshop and realized your potential as a digital artist, going from a novice to a competent one.

Keeping that in mind, this is just the beginning. As you learn new tricks and start fascinating projects, your newly acquired talents, and knowledge will keep expanding. So continue honing your skills, trying new things, and stretching your creative abilities.

I appreciate you being a part of this life-changing adventure. Now, go out and continue to produce stunning digital art with confidence and zeal!

To build a strong foundation in Photoshop and position yourself for success in Book 2, we recommend that you study "Photoshop for Beginners" (Book 1) if you haven't already. Get Photoshop for Beginners (Book 3) to continue your exploration and expand your knowledge.